How To Use This Study Guide

This five-lesson study guide corresponds to *"Demystifying the Prophetic" With Rick Renner and Guest Joseph Z* (Renner TV). Each lesson in this study guide covers a topic that is addressed during the program series, with questions and references supplied to draw you deeper into your own private study of the Scriptures on this subject.

To derive the most benefit from this study guide, consider the following:

First, watch or listen to the program prior to working through the corresponding lesson in this guide. (Programs can also be viewed at **renner.org** by clicking on the Media/Archives links or on our Renner Ministries YouTube channel.)

Second, take the time to look up the scriptures included in each lesson. Prayerfully consider their application to your own life.

Third, use a journal or notebook to make note of your answers to each lesson's Study Questions and Practical Application challenges.

Fourth, invest specific time in prayer and in the Word of God to consult with the Holy Spirit. Write down the scriptures or insights He reveals to you.

Finally, take action! Whatever the Lord tells you to do according to His Word, do it.

For added insights on this subject, it is recommended that you obtain Joseph Z's book *Demystifying the Prophetic: Understanding the Voice of God for the Coming Days of Fire* and Rick Renner's book *Fallen Angels, Giants, Monsters, and the World Before the Flood*. You may also select from Rick's other available resources by placing your order at **renner.org** or by calling 1-800-742-5593.

TOPIC

God Speaks From the Spirit Realm

SCRIPTURES

No scriptures were shown in the program in this lesson.

GREEK WORDS

No Greek Words were shown in the programs in this series.

SYNOPSIS

In this lesson, Rick and Joseph Z address the confusion caused by an extreme emphasis on the prophetic ministry in recent years. By referencing Joseph Z's book *Demystifying the Prophetic*, they discuss the importance of rightsizing the prophetic movement with a balanced view from the Word of God. The Bible admonishes believers not to despise prophesying, so we must gain a proper understanding of prophecy instead of throwing it out completely. When we operate in prophecy correctly, it is a great blessing to the Body of Christ.

The five lessons in this study on *Demystifying the Prophetic* will focus on the following topics:

- God Speaks From the Spirit Realm
- 4 Types of Prophecy — the Prophetic Spectrum
- Revelation, Interpretation, Application
- Navigating Prophetic Experiences
- Solving Prophetic Enigmas

The emphasis of this lesson:

Many in the Church have been confused, turned off, and even disgusted by the prophetic excess and extremism running rampant today. Thankfully the Word of God can bring order and balance to the supernatural. When believers become familiar with God's Word on the subject of

A Note From Rick Renner

I am on a personal quest to see a "revival of the Bible" so people can establish their lives on a firm foundation that will stand strong and endure the test as end-time storm winds begin to intensify.

In order to experience a revival of the Bible in your personal life, it is important to take time each day to read, receive, and apply its truths to your life. James tells us that if we will continue in the perfect law of liberty — refusing to be forgetful hearers, but determined to be doers — we will be blessed in our ways. As you watch or listen to the programs in this series and work through this corresponding study guide, I trust you will search the Scriptures and allow the Holy Spirit to help you hear something new from God's Word that applies specifically to your life. I encourage you to be a doer of the Word He reveals to you. Whatever the cost, I assure you — it will be worth it.

> Thy words were found, and I did eat them;
> and thy word was unto me the joy and rejoicing of mine heart:
> for I am called by thy name, O Lord God of hosts.
> — Jeremiah 15:16

Your brother and friend in Jesus Christ,

Rick Renner

Unless otherwise indicated, all scripture quotations are taken from the *King James Version* of the Bible.

Scripture quotations marked (*NKJV*) are taken from the *New King James Version*®. Copyright © 1982 by Thomas Nelson. Used by permission. All rights reserved.

Demystifying the Prophetic

Copyright © 2024 by Rick Renner
1814 W. Tacoma St.
Broken Arrow, OK 74012-1406

Published by Rick Renner Ministries
www.renner.org

ISBN 13: 978-1-6675-0907-5

ISBN 13 eBook: 978-1-6675-0908-2

All rights reserved. No portion of this book may be reproduced or transmitted in any form or by any means — electronic, mechanical, photocopy, recording, scanning, or other — except for brief quotations in critical reviews or articles, without the prior written permission of the Publisher.

Rick Renner's guest during this series is Joseph Z, founder of Z Ministries. Joseph is an international prophetic voice who builds lives by the Word of God in the church, government, and marketplace. He and his wife Heather currently reside in Colorado Springs, CO, with their two children. For more information, visit **josephz.com**.

prophecy and how prophecy is to be judged, they can walk in proper biblical discernment and maturity.

Introduction to Prophetic Ministry

In recent years, there has been an increasing amount of interest and emphasis on the gift of prophecy, the ministry office of the prophet, and prophetic ministry. With all the different voices and experiences out there, many believers have had difficulties discerning what prophecies are truly from the Lord. The prophetic craze has swung to such wild extremes that anything labeled prophetic has now left a bad taste in the mouths of many in the Body of Christ.

While there has been much confusion, excess, and error in the prophetic movement, the Bible says that we are not to despise prophecy. The supernatural gifts of the spirit are still needed in the Church, and there is a genuine operation of the prophet's five-fold gift in New Testament ministry. Therefore, the proper response to the present prophetic chaos is to return to the Word of God and discover the biblical foundations, boundaries, qualifications, and guidelines for prophecy, prophetic ministry, and the prophet's office.

In reference to his book, *Demystifying the Supernatural,* Joseph Z calls attention to the need for "right-sizing" the prophetic ministry and bringing it back into proper alignment according to the Bible. As he points out, one of the first things we need to understand about prophecy is that God is a Spirit. He exists in the spirit realm, and that's where we connect with Him.

There has also been some confusion about the difference between how prophecy operated in the Old Testament and how it operates today under the new covenant. In the Old Testament, before the death, burial, and resurrection of Jesus, the only access Jews had to God was through the prophet, priest, and king. The prophetic manifestations were rather dramatic because the Holy Spirit had not yet come to live inside believers. With the new birth came the indwelling presence of the Holy Spirit, which altered some of the prophetic demonstrations. Instead of always looking for outward, natural manifestations to show us the way, we now can listen to the voice of the Holy Spirit speaking to us from inside our spirits.

Although every believer has the Holy Spirit inside him, he must still develop his spiritual ear to hear the voice of the Holy Spirit speaking to him. It takes time to train our spirits to become sensitive to His voice, and it's a lifelong process of growing up spiritually in our walk with the Lord.

To help us understand Him and discern His voice properly, God gave us His Word. The more we anchor ourselves in the Bible, the easier it is for us to recognize His voice in the spiritual realm. When we have questions about a particular prophecy or spiritual manifestation, we need to line it up against the Bible to measure its accuracy. Judging prophecy by the Word of God is the primary way to discern if a prophecy is truly from the Lord.

When a prophecy isn't genuinely inspired by the Holy Spirit, we may have a sense that something seems off. It's important to pay attention to those red flags by scrutinizing even more carefully whatever we've heard that seems amiss. Everything must be tested by God's Word.

To become familiar with God's voice, we must spend time — *every day* — reading God's Word until it begins impacting our decisions, thoughts, actions, and words. We should read the Bible so much that it starts "talking back to us"! Daily time in God's Word begins to shape our discernment of how God acts, what He thinks, what He does, and how we can live in a way that is pleasing to Him.

Bringing Order to the Prophetic

In rightsizing the prophetic, we must understand that even genuine prophets make mistakes sometimes. Just because someone misses it doesn't necessarily mean he is a "false prophet." No one is perfect, and we are all growing in our maturity and accuracy.

Listening to others in the Body is key to helping us stay in balance. If we make a mistake regarding prophecy, it is an opportunity for humility and self-correction. However, failing to make adjustments once correction comes can continue to fortify a wrong perception, wrong teaching, and wrong mode of operation. This is a dangerous path that can lead many astray!

Another key to bringing order to the prophetic is understanding that some prophecies are missed by a technicality. In other words, the exact details may not have been completely accurate, but the message was right.

A biblical example of this is found in Acts 15 when Agabus prophesied to Paul about being bound by the Jews. As it turned out, Paul was indeed bound — but not by Jews. He was arrested by the Romans. So while it appeared Agabus missed it, he only missed it by a technicality. The message he gave Paul was correct as a whole.

True prophecy will also glorify Jesus and confirm what's already in our hearts. It will leave us with a spirit of faith and not a sense of fear or dread. As an example of this truth, Rick shared a story that happened to him several years ago. Someone had prophesied to him that he was to never get on a plane again because of a possible crash. That word did not confirm what he had in his heart because the particular call of his ministry required him to travel. Since he knew that word was not from the Lord, he disregarded it and continued on in faith in his ministry travels.

When it comes to prophecy, we need to be on guard against sensationalism and religious traditions. Prophecy does not have to involve spectacular pageantry or follow any particular traditional approach. However, it does need to present a clear word that is balanced by Scripture.

One thing that helps set the tone for the moving of the gifts of the Spirit — including prophecy — is worship. Music that magnifies Jesus not only moves our attention from natural things to spiritual things, but it can also help usher in the manifested presence of God. It is during these times of worship that the Holy Spirit will often demonstrate Himself with a prophetic utterance or other gifts of the Spirit.

Of course, praying in tongues is also a key element to preparing our hearts to hear from the Lord. It helps us put up our spiritual antennas so that we can better hear what the Holy Spirit is speaking. By praying in our heavenly language, we are making ourselves available as a conduit to hear the voice of God.

As we anchor ourselves in the Word of God, we can learn to distinguish the difference between true and false prophetic ministry. There is room for correction and maturity in all of us if we will receive God's rightsizing in our lives. True prophecy inspired by the Holy Spirit is a gift from God and is needed in the Church today!

QUESTIONS AND ANSWERS WITH RICK RENNER

In the program, Rick answered the following question from one of our viewers.

Q. Will persecution come to America and to the Western world?

A. "Well, my friend, it's already here. But Jesus answered this question about the end times in Luke 21:12, where He said, 'But before all these [things], they shall lay their hands on you...,' which describes physical arrest; '...and persecute you...,' which means they're going to legally pursue you; '...and delivering you up to the synagogues, and into prisons, being brought before kings and rulers for my name's sake.'"

"The word *synagogues* here is very important because in the Jewish world, the synagogue was also the legal court system for the Jews. And here Jesus is prophesying that at the very end of the age, the court system will become weaponized against believers and those who take a stand for the truth, which places them opposite to what is taking place in the world system. So that is Jesus' answer about what's going to happen in the end of the age."

STUDY QUESTIONS

Study to shew thyself approved unto God, a workman that needeth not to be ashamed, rightly dividing the word of truth.
— 2 Timothy 2:15

1. First Thessalonians 5:20 says, "Despise not prophesyings." Have you ever been tempted to despise prophecy because of excess or error regarding prophetic ministry?

2. First Corinthians 14:3 says, "But he that prophesieth speaketh unto men to edification, and exhortation, and comfort." What prophecies have you heard that match up with this scripture test?

3. Ephesians 4:32 says, "And be ye kind one to another, tenderhearted, forgiving one another, even as God for Christ's sake hath forgiven you." If you've been angry at another brother or sister in the Lord who may have missed it regarding a prophetic word, how are you letting the Word of God govern you? Are you being kind and tenderhearted toward that person? Are you walking in forgiveness and extending mercy to those who missed it?

PRACTICAL APPLICATION

> But be ye doers of the word, and not hearers only,
> deceiving your own selves.
> —James 1:22

Learn to judge prophecy by the Word.

1. When you hear a prophecy, how do you judge it by God's Word?
2. Can you think of a time when you heard a prophecy that didn't seem right? What made it seem off to you, and how did you discern it by the Word of God?
3. When you've heard a genuine prophecy, how did it confirm what was in your heart?

LESSON 2

TOPIC

4 Types of Prophecy — the Prophetic Spectrum

SCRIPTURES

1. **1 Chronicles 29:29** — Now in the acts of David the king, first and last, behold, they are written in the book of Samuel the seer, and in the book of Nathan the prophet, and in the book of Gad the seer.
2. **2 Kings 8:10-12** (*NKJV*) — And Elisha said to him, "Go, say to him, 'You shall certainly recover.' However the Lord has shown me that he will really die." Then he set his countenance in a stare until he was ashamed; and the man of God wept. And Hazael said, "Why is my lord weeping?" He answered, "Because I know the evil that you will do to the children of Israel: Their strongholds you will set on fire, and their young men you will kill with the sword; and you will dash their children, and rip open their women with child."
3. **Ezekiel 12:27** (*NKJV*) — "Son of man, look, the house of Israel is saying, 'The vision that he sees is for many days from now, and he prophesies of times far off.'"

SYNOPSIS

In this lesson, Rick and Joseph Z continue their conversation about prophecy and prophetic experiences. Using insight from Joseph's book *Demystifying the Prophetic*, they discuss the difference between the prophet's office and the simple gift of prophecy. They dive into four specific prophetic flows described in the Old Testament and show how these distinctions are still visible in the office of the prophet today.

The emphasis of this lesson:

The Old Testament notes four specific prophetic flows that are key to interpreting different operations within the prophet's office. From these examples in Scripture, believers can better understand how the prophetic ministry functions while still maintaining scriptural integrity.

Understanding the Different Types of Prophets and Prophecy

As we learn about prophecy from God's Word, it's important for us to first discern the difference between a prophet and the simple gift of prophecy. Although prophets do prophesy, not all who prophesy are called to the prophet's office. In simplest terms, a prophet is someone who stands in the five-fold ministry and has a responsibility to the Body of Christ. On the other hand, the simple gift of prophecy is available for every Spirit-filled believer.

In the Old Testament, we see a particular distinction between four different kinds of prophetic flows: *roeh, nabi, chazah,* and *chozeh*. These can be major or minor strengths in the operation of a prophet's ministry. Together, these four prophetic flows can help us better understand how one prophet may function in his gift differently from another called to the same ministry office.

Three of the four types of prophetic flows are mentioned in First Chronicles 29:29: "Now the acts of David the king, first and last, behold, they are written in the book of Samuel the **seer**, and in the book of Nathan the **prophet**, and in the book of Gad the **seer**." The first type of prophetic flow mentioned in this verse is "seer," or the Hebrew word *roeh*, which describes a visionary prophetic gift. This is *someone who sees or knows what to do in a particular situation or environment*. Because of his visual perception, he intuitively knows what actions need to be executed to fulfill a desired outcome.

An example of *roeh* is found in First Chronicles 12:32. The sons of Issachar knew the signs of the times. Not only could they understand them, but they also knew what to do about them. They knew who they were to be aligned with and what actions needed to be taken in light of the times.

The second prophetic flow is *nabi*, the Hebrew word for "prophet." This is the most common form of the prophetic, and it means a *bubbling up*. *Nabi* describes someone who declares and gives information much like a herald — like a trumpet. It is an inspirational gift that can be demonstrated when a minister begins to extemporaneously speak from the Word of God as it bubbles up inside him. The inspired message declares, forthtells, foretells the future, or what's happening.

The third flow is *chazah*, which can also be translated as "seer." However, its connotation varies from *roeh*, as it means *to look and to continue to look*. It can also mean *to gaze*. The manifestation of *chazah* can be seen in the story of Elisha when he stared at Hazael and saw that he would do evil to the children of Israel (*see* 2 Kings 8:10-12). In this instance, Elisha was gazing into the spirit realm until he saw something revealed to him by the Spirit of God.

The fourth flow, *chozeh* or "vision" comes from Ezekiel 12:27 (*NKJV*): "Son of man, look, the house of Israel is saying, 'The vision that he sees is for many days from now, and he prophesies of times far off.'" *Chozeh* means *to peer forward* into the future or to *lean into and look into* the distance. It's a futurist prophetic gift that is sometimes manifested in trances, dreams, or profound visions. Another example of the manifestation of this flow can be seen in the life of Daniel, John the Revelator, and Gad, a prophet in the time of King David.

While all four prophetic experiences are necessary and powerful, the key to maintaining a balanced prophetic ministry is to interpret all prophetic experiences in light of God's Word. Because God is a Spirit, He does move in the realm of the spirit and provides information and insight to us by the Holy Spirit through the gifts of the Spirit, prophecy, and prophetic flows. No matter how magnificent a spiritual experience may seem, it still must be scripturally examined. A good rule of thumb to remember is this: Prophetic experience never supersedes the Word of God!

QUESTIONS AND ANSWERS WITH RICK RENNER

In the program, Rick answered the following question from one of our viewers.

Q. What's going to happen in Heaven during the Great Tribulation?

A. "We know that the great tribulation will begin when the Church is raptured, and I'm a firm believer in the rapture of the Church. As soon as we are vacated, God's wrath will begin to be poured out on the earth for seven years.

"But while God's wrath is being poured out on the earth, a lot of activity is going to be happening in Heaven. We're going to be attending the Marriage Feast of the Lamb. According to Second Corinthians 5:10, during those seven years, each of us will stand before the Judgment Seat of Christ and give account for our level of obedience in this life.

"Our future occupation in eternity will be determined by how faithful we are now, which means this is a qualifying time for what we're going to do in the future. If you want to do something wonderful in eternity, then God needs to find you faithful now. During the Great Tribulation, Heaven is going to be filled with activity as we celebrate with the Lord at the Marriage Feast of the Lamb and as each one of us is called singularly before the Judgment Seat of Christ to receive our reward for our levels of obedience."

STUDY QUESTIONS

> Study to shew thyself approved unto God, a workman that needeth
> not to be ashamed, rightly dividing the word of truth.
> — 2 Timothy 2:15

1. How does learning about the four unique prophetic flows help you better understand prophetic experiences or demonstrations?

2. Ephesians 4:11 says, "And he gave some, apostles; and some, prophets; and some, evangelists; and some, pastors and teachers." According to this scripture, the prophet's office is one of the five-fold ministry gifts. What ministers do you know who walk in the prophet's ministry office?

3. First Corinthians 12:10 lists prophecy as one of the gifts of the Spirit. Can you name the other gifts mentioned in First Corinthians 12?

PRACTICAL APPLICATION

> But be ye doers of the word, and not hearers only,
> deceiving your own selves.
> — James 1:22

Stay balanced in your spiritual experiences.

1. Define the four types of prophetic flows discussed in this chapter.
2. Have you ever had a spiritual experience that you didn't understand? How did you examine it from Scripture?
3. Has someone shared with you a spiritual experience that didn't line up with Scripture? How did you respond?

TOPIC

Revelation, Interpretation, Application

SCRIPTURES

1. **Acts 15:28** (*NKJV*) — For it seemed good to the Holy Spirit, and to us, to lay upon you no greater burden than these necessary things.
2. **James 1:23,24** (*NKJV*) — For if anyone is a hearer of the word and not a doer, he is like a man observing his natural face in a mirror; for he observes himself, goes away, and immediately forgets what kind of man he was.
3. **Hebrews 5:14** (*NKJV*) — But solid food belongs to those who are of full age, that is, those who by reason of use have their senses exercised to discern both good and evil.

SYNOPSIS

In this lesson, Rick and Joseph continue their conversation about rightsizing the prophetic. They address some concerns about prophetic extremism operating in the Church today and how to correct it through a balanced biblical view. Joseph then discusses three vital keys to understanding any word of prophecy. By honoring others in the Body, believers can begin piecing together the prophetic mysteries to obtain a more comprehensive view of end-time events.

The emphasis of this lesson:

Due to an extreme emphasis on the prophetic in recent years, many believers have become skeptical about the gift of prophecy and prophetic ministry. To bring balance and clarity to the issue, believers need to understand how prophecy should be received and processed. When a proper hermeneutic framework is applied to prophecy, believers can untangle the confusion in their minds and walk in the blessing of biblically balanced prophecy.

Prophetic Extremism

In today's spiritual landscape, there is an overemphasis on the prophetic that has led to much confusion, extremism, error, and excess. YouTube is filled with nutty "wannabe" prophets, sensationalism dominates the headlines, and failed political predictions litter the scene. Because there is a lack of solid teaching and guidance in this area, many believers are being misled in their zeal for prophetic experiences, prophecy, and the supernatural. Sadly, the result of such confusion is causing many to become unbalanced in their doctrine and shipwrecked in their faith.

To correct this chaos and not grow to despise prophecy (*see* 1 Thessalonians 5:20,21), we desperately need biblical rightsizing to the prophetic movement. There needs to be more personal accountability, proper interpretation, and a wariness of the sensational. Unfortunately, many who operate in the gift of prophecy feel the need to have something new all the time. That pressure to perform has catered to the market for the outlandish, which has only intensified the confusion.

The key to finding the center is returning to the Word of God for counsel, correction, and context for the supernatural. Many have sensed something in their spirits, but because they didn't have a foundation in the Word of God, they jumped ahead and missed God on the timing or interpretation of prophecy. By building a proper biblical foundation for prophecy, we can all make the necessary adjustments and move forward in the right, balanced direction.

Revelation, Interpretation, Application

According to Joseph Z, there are three keys that will help balance out the extremes in the prophetic: *revelation, interpretation,* and *application.* By correcting these three areas, Joseph believes we can operate in a better hermeneutic framework (the art and science of interpretation) for prophecy.

The first step is understanding *revelation* properly. A revelation is the moment of a supernatural encounter. It's when the light bulb goes on in our spirits, and something suddenly explodes inside us. Our mind has just become illuminated — it's an "aha" moment. This can happen anytime — when we're reading our Bible, praying, worshiping, listening to a message, or just in a meeting.

Interestingly, the Greek word for "illumination" is *photidzo,* which is where we get the word for a photograph. So when we have a divine illumination, it's like a brilliant flash of light capturing a permanent impression on our spirits. Information or knowledge is supernaturally revealed to us in a moment of time.

When we receive this instant illumination or revelation, we then have to process this information properly. It is at this point of processing the revelation that many people miss it and make mistakes. Instead of waiting on God and getting His correct timing and interpretation on a matter, they just run after that revelation. They do exactly what they see photographed in their spirits and don't wait for the development of that revelation.

This is why the second step — *interpretation* — is so vital. Without proper interpretation of the revelation, we will miss whatever it is God has spoken to us. Acts 15:28 says, "For it seemed good to the Holy Spirit, and to us...." Revelation is vital, but then we have to go to the mirror of God's Word and not walk away forgetting what we've seen (*see* James 1:23,24).

Interpretation has a lot to do with the execution of timing. Usually, when God shows us something by revelation, He doesn't mean for us to do it *now.* He's simply showing us the destination for our future, and it's up to us to discern the proper interpretation or timing of that particular revelation.

In the program, Joseph shared an instance in his life when the Lord spoke to him and said, "I am calling you to full-time ministry." That same weekend, another prophet came to him and told him the same thing. Not too long after that, another prophet spoke the same word to him, "The Lord is calling you to leave work and go into full-time ministry."

Since Joseph had received the revelation and two confirmations, he immediately quit his job. But in doing so, he missed God's timing of the word given to him. Joseph confessed that he should have prayed and walked out the process of that revelation. Had he stayed at his job a little longer, he would have received six months of severance pay when the company closed. Because he didn't understand the interpretation of the revelation, he stepped out of time early and missed God's proper plan. What he saw was right, but his timing was wrong.

This brings us to the third step of understanding prophecy correctly and that is application — knowing what you ought to do and when you ought to do it. Application is doing the revelation with the interpretation at the right time, with the right people, and with common sense. When we connect all three pieces together — revelation, interpretation, and application — we can walk into the fullness of what God said with the exact results He desires.

Hebrews 5:14 instructs, "…Those who by reason of use have their senses exercised to discern both good and evil." When revelation is received and interpreted correctly, the recipient of the revelation will know when to walk in it and when to apply what has been heard.

Complements and Contradictions

On occasion, it may seem that two different prophecies actually contradict themselves. But if we dive deeper below the surface, we may be surprised to discover that what first appeared as a contradiction was actually a complement and confirmation! Both prophecies may have been correct, but because they each emphasized a different perspective on the same situation, it may look like both were wrong.

The Old Testament provides one such example of apparent conflicting prophetic words. Both Ezekiel and Jeremiah had a word for King Zedekiah. One told Zedekiah that he would not see the Babylonian invasion (*see* Ezekiel 12:8-13), while the other told him he would indeed go to Babylon (*see* Jeremiah 34:3). At first, it seemed as if the two prophecies were contradictions.

It wasn't until the actual event took place that the prophecies were accurately understood. Once Babylon invaded Jerusalem, the Babylonian king captured Zedekiah. They gouged out his eyes and then led him to Babylon. Each prophet had a piece of the puzzle that, when put together, formed the complete picture. In fulfillment of both complementing prophecies, it happened that Zedekiah was taken to Babylon, but he didn't see the Babylonian invasion because he lost his eyesight.

This story illustrates the importance of connecting different prophecies and recognizing how they paint a fuller picture when put together. God may give a certain person one piece of the puzzle, and then He'll give another a separate piece of the same puzzle. At first glance, it may not seem like the pieces fit together. But if we'll wait for proper interpretation and application of the revelation, we can see a more comprehensive picture of what the Lord is saying to His people. This is why we need each other in the Body of Christ!

The Bible tells us that we prophesy in part. This means that when we receive something from the Lord, we may not have all the full details of one particular revelation. It's just a part or a piece of a larger puzzle.

Another such example can be found in Acts 21. The apostle Paul was traveling and ministering, and he stayed several days at the house of Philip the evangelist. Philip had four daughters, all of whom had the gift of prophecy, but it wasn't until the prophet Agabus arrived that a word from the Lord for Paul was given. In this instance, Agabus saw what the other prophets did not, and they made room for his gift.

In order to work together in prophetic unity in the Body, we need to understand that each piece is important. This requires humility and cooperation among the members of the Body. When one has a piece, he can speak. And when he's finished, he can sit down, be quiet, and listen to the others speak what the Lord has given them. As a result of this type of honor and deference, we can gain a broader, deeper, and clearer understanding of what God wants to do in these last days.

QUESTIONS AND ANSWERS WITH RICK RENNER

In the program, Rick answered the following question from one of our viewers.

Q. Why do people sometimes collapse in the presence of the Lord?

A. "Let's look at Revelation 1:17, where the apostle John on the isle of Patmos saw the exalted Christ and John responded in a particular fashion: 'And when I saw him, I fell at his feet dead....' That particular word for 'fall' means *to collapse*, which means his legs literally buckled underneath him and he collapsed. The word 'dead' is the Greek word *nekros*, which is where we get the word 'corpse.' John literally meant that his feet buckled underneath him, and he collapsed on the ground like a dead man.

"Sometimes when we come in contact with the power of God, it is so strong that something's got to give — and that may mean our legs! They may buckle underneath us causing us to collapse on the ground under the power of God. By the way, when we're lying under the power of God, He is doing some kind of supernatural work in us.

"This is why people sometimes collapse in the presence of God."

STUDY QUESTIONS

> **Study to shew thyself approved unto God, a workman that needeth not to be ashamed, rightly dividing the word of truth.**
> **— 2 Timothy 2:15**

1. Acts 15:28 says, "For it seemed good to the Holy Spirit, and to us, to lay upon you no greater burden than these necessary things." When you've tried to do something God told you to do, did you sense a peace in your spirit? Or was there something that didn't seem quite right in your heart because your timing was off?

2. James 1:23 and 24 says, "For if anyone is a hearer of the word and not a doer, he is like a man observing his natural face in a mirror; for he observes himself, goes away, and immediately forgets what kind of man he was." In light of this scripture, have you received a word from God but needed to spend time in the Bible to properly discern God's plan and His development process in you?

3. Prior to this lesson, were you aware of the two seemingly contradicting prophecies regarding King Zedekiah?

PRACTICAL APPLICATION

But be ye doers of the word, and not hearers only,
deceiving your own selves.
— James 1:22

Allow God's revelation to unfold fully.

1. What prophecies have you heard that seemed contradictory? Have you ever considered how they may be complementary in their foretelling of a bigger, more comprehensive picture?
2. When have you received a revelation or illumination in your spirit, and how did you act upon that word? Did you take time to wait on God in study and prayer to discern His proper plan of execution, or did you run after that word without any thought of God's timing and process?
3. Can you think of a time when you missed God's timing in your life? How did that mistake impact the plan you saw in your heart?

LESSON 4

TOPIC

Navigating Prophetic Experiences

SCRIPTURES

No scriptures were shown in the program in this lesson.

SYNOPSIS

In this lesson, Rick and Joseph continue their conversation about demystifying the prophetic. They discuss how navigating the supernatural is much like navigating the terrain on a map. With the help of the Holy Spirit, a strong foundation in God's Word, and some common sense, believers can successfully interpret what God is speaking to the Church today.

The emphasis of this lesson:

Without the compass of the Holy Spirit and the guidebook of the Word of God, navigating the prophetic can become quite challenging! But God is not the God of confusion — He's the God of clarity and peace. If believers will approach spiritual experiences with a biblical framework and common sense, they won't get lost in excess or extremism.

The Map Is Not the Territory

As we continue to work with God's rightsizing of the prophetic, we must understand that experiences are often subjective. This is why every prophecy or spiritual experience must be subject to the Word of God. The Bible is what will give us the proper framework for interpreting the prophetic accurately. It will also keep us safe from veering off into wrong doctrine, sensationalism, or even familiar spirits.

God is not the author of confusion. He's given us His Word to help us navigate the spiritual realm in accuracy, holiness, and alignment with His plans and purposes. Prophecy and the other gifts of the Spirit are given to us for clarity, not for confusion. By following God's boundaries in His Word, we can rightly discern any spiritual experience and receive what the Holy Spirit is saying to us. Joseph Z has a saying: "The tongue of the uninspired is criticism, but the native tongue of God is clarity." Prophecy is clarification — so we can hear what He is saying to us.

As one man once said, "The map is not the territory." Spiritual experiences can be likened to a map — the map represents a territory, but it is not the actual territory. In other words, a spiritual experience gives us a sense of what may be on the horizon, but it's not the thing itself. It's only a snapshot of what is coming. The only hard evidence we can build our life on is the actual written Word of God. Without that sound foundation, spiritual experiences can lead us off track.

Moreover, when we arrive at the destination we saw in the spirit, it can sometimes look very different from what we originally perceived, because we only saw a portion of it. Again, the Bible tells us that we prophesy in part. This means that when the Holy Spirit shows us something, He gives us a small portion of a bigger picture.

If we don't have our mind and soul balanced by the Word of God, we can even misinterpret the small part that the Holy Spirit did show us. In relation to prophecy, the Bible also teaches that we see through a glass dimly (*see* 1 Corinthians 13:12). If our soul is off in an area, it can color the way we view things and make the glass dimmer than it should be. The more we step into the Word of God, the more we polish the glass of our soul. As a result, we can gain a clearer understanding of our spiritual experiences.

Being Led by the Holy Spirit

Another aspect of navigating the terrain of prophecy properly is being led by the Holy Spirit. This requires us to develop our spirits to hear the voice of God accurately. Spiritual growth and development come by studying God's Word and doing what it says.

Prophecy is a sensory compass; it's not just based on facts, rote repetition, or even every word the Bible says. There's also a sensory aspect to it, and that is being led. For example, the Bible doesn't tell us who to marry or when to go on vacation. But the Spirit of God can show us what we need to know. That's the sensory part.

Sometimes when we're being led by the Holy Spirit there's a check or a restriction in our hearts not to go in a certain way. The apostle Paul had this experience in Acts 16 when he tried to go into a few different areas to preach the Gospel but was forbidden or restricted by the Holy Spirit. Something in his spirit didn't feel right about the situation. There was a restriction or a sense that he shouldn't go in that direction.

One way to keep our spirits sensitive to the leading of the Holy Spirit is to pray in other tongues. When we pray in tongues, we pray out the mysteries of God (*see* 1 Corinthians 14:2). Over time, those mysteries we've prayed out in the Spirit begin to connect with our understanding and become revelation. We then get a sense of what we need to do in a certain area. As we continue to press into that place of prayer, our mental and soulish alignment begins to shift to our heart. Then the mysteries of God become clearer and clearer to us until we know God's precise plan.

Again, Hebrews 5:14 informs us, "…Those who by reason of use have their senses exercised to discern both good and evil." When we renew our mind to God's Word and the Holy Spirit (*see* Romans 12:12), it takes all our natural faculties — including our five senses — and puts them under the authority of the Word of God.

The Wisdom of Using Common Sense

Another important key in navigating the terrain is using common sense. This is where many people make mistakes and get off onto the wrong path. God doesn't ask us to do nonsensical things that will get us into trouble later on.

You may experience unique and interesting prophetic moments in your life, but a genuine prophetic experience will always agree with the Word of God — always. The testimony of Jesus is the spirit of prophecy (*see* Revelation 19:10), so the spirit of prophecy gives testimony of Jesus. In other words, whatever is happening when the voice of God is speaking, whatever is happening by the flow of the Spirit, will always give glory to Jesus. So any "prophetic" word that leaves you in fear, trepidation, anxiety, or just stuck, that's probably *not* a word from the Lord.

By staying the course with the Word of God, we can safely navigate the terrain of prophecy and spiritual experiences. If we've missed it in times past, we can repent, make the corrections, and move on with a more solid framework that comes from the Bible. The map of prophecy doesn't have to be confusing! With the help of the Holy Spirit, common sense, and a strong foundation in the Word, we can successfully reach the destination God has for us.

QUESTIONS AND ANSWERS WITH RICK RENNER

In the program, Rick answered the following question from one of our viewers.

Q. What is "lashon hara"?

A. "Whoever asked that question knows something about the Jews, because 'lashon hara' was a term used among the Jews to describe *evil speaking*. It was the equivalent of 'thou shalt not kill.' Wow!

"Why was it the equivalent of killing? Because when you speak evil of someone else, you assassinate their character. When others hear you, it ruins the reputation of that person in the minds and ears of those who are listening. Even if you change your mind, it is impossible to go back to every single person with whom you've spoken evil about that individual and retract what you said. Therefore, it is considered the equivalent of killing or character assassination. Friends, we need to be very careful what we do with our mouths and be certain that we do not participate in *lashon hara*."

STUDY QUESTIONS

> Study to shew thyself approved unto God, a workman that needeth
> not to be ashamed, rightly dividing the word of truth.
> — 2 Timothy 2:15

1. Hebrews 5:14 says, "…Those who by reason of use have their senses exercised to discern both good and evil." How are you letting the Word of God sharpen your spirit so that you're able to discern genuine prophecy?

2. Romans 12:2 says, "And do not be conformed to this world, but be transformed by the renewing of your mind, that you may prove what is that good and acceptable and perfect will of God." How has staying in the Word of God affected your thinking in a particular area?

3. Acts 16 records instances in Paul's journey when the Holy Spirit restricted him from preaching the Gospel in certain regions. When was the last time the Holy Spirit restricted you from doing something? Did you obey His leading?

PRACTICAL APPLICATION

> But be ye doers of the word, and not hearers only,
> deceiving your own selves.
> — James 1:22

Navigate the terrain with God's Word and common sense.

1. Were you ever confused by a prophetic experience? Did you go to the Word to discern that experience properly?

2. Have you ever had the Lord show you something about your future, but it looked completely different by the time you got there? How did you respond?

3. What does the Word say about using common sense? (*See* Proverbs 19:8 *ESV*; Proverbs 2:7-17 *NLT*; and Proverbs 3:21-20 *NLT*.) Have you ever made mistakes in an attempt to do something for God but later realized you should have used some common sense as you set out on your journey?

TOPIC

Solving Prophetic Enigmas

SCRIPTURES

1. **1 Corinthians 13:9** — For we know in part, and we prophesy in part.
2. **1 Corinthians 13:12** — For we now see through a glass, darkly; but then face to face: now I know in part; but then shall I know even as also I am known.

SYNOPSIS

In this lesson, Rick and Joseph Z wrap up their conversation about prophecy in the Church today, and discuss how different pieces of prophecy can act as clues to the greater picture God is showing His people. By using biblical discernment while honoring others in the Body, believers can work together to solve this spiritual puzzle or enigma.

The emphasis of this lesson:

The Bible tells us that we know in part, and we prophesy in part. This principle of prophecy can be likened to a giant, spiritual jigsaw puzzle with many different pieces being distributed to several members across the Body of Christ. To solve the puzzle, we have to examine each piece carefully using a proper biblical framework. Once we bring all the pieces together, we can gain a better understanding of the full revelation the Holy Spirit is speaking to the Church today.

Putting the Pieces Together

When it comes to solving prophetic enigmas, First Corinthians 13:9 gives us valuable insight: "For we know in part, and we prophesy in part." Translated from the Greek words *ek meros*, the phrase "in part" means *to know in pieces*. When we prophesy, the Holy Spirit is only showing us one particular aspect of a much larger message. It takes all the parts coming together to solve the mystery.

Each of us has our part that we are to know really well. But we have to work together to understand the full scope of what the Holy Spirit is speaking to His Body. This means we must learn to listen to one another, honor the gifts in one another, and cooperate with the rest of the Body of Christ to hear everything God wants us to hear.

Understanding prophecy is much like assembling a giant jigsaw puzzle. To put the pieces together properly, we start with the clearly defined edge pieces. Once the framework is complete, we work on the middle portion and then build out our puzzle from there. It's only when we bring all the pieces together that the picture is complete.

Similarly, it takes all of us coming together with our pieces to receive the whole counsel of God. By walking in humility and appreciating the gifts in one another, we can begin to discern the bigger picture God is showing His Body. Together, we solve the puzzle.

It's an Enigma

First Corinthians 13:12 goes on to say, "For now we see through a glass darkly." The word "darkly" in the Greek is pronounced *enigma*. In other words, when we see something in the spirit, we see only a portion of an enigma, puzzle, or riddle. It's a clue to the mystery!

In the program, to illustrate the meaning of "glass" in this verse, Rick brings out a deep-blue slag of Roman glass. When he holds it up to the light, we can see bursts of light coming through, but it's not clear. We can't see through the glass to the other side. Sometimes our knowledge and prophetic ministry is like that; we see bursts of light where we know God is saying something to us, but we may not see the picture clearly. It's a little bit of an enigma to us.

Rick then brings out an ancient Roman mirror made out of metal — the second meaning of the word "glass." To see a proper reflection, he has to shine it and bring it up to the light and look at it from several different angles. Similarly, we must look at prophecy closely from many different angles until the blurriness fades and the full picture comes into clear focus.

We end up making mistakes with prophecy when we fail to examine it from multiple angles. It takes all the pieces coming together to understand the complex revelation in its entirety. Therefore, it's critical to develop discernment before taking action.

Shining the Light of the Word of God

Another key to solving prophetic enigmas is to shine the light of God's Word on prophecy. The more we stay in God's Word, the more adequately we can discern God's voice, His character, and His ways. By prioritizing God's Word in our daily life, our senses are exercised to know the difference between right and wrong. It's not a matter of intelligence or mental acuity — the Word of God has the ability to develop discernment in us.

With the serious geo-political implications of the days we live in, it's important for each of us to consider carefully the different prophecies we may hear. We can't just swallow everything we see and hear on YouTube, because many voices out there are out of orbit. The Bible tells us we are to know those who labor among us (*see* 1 Thessalonians 5:12). We should be cautious with voices we're unfamiliar with and diligently search out what they represent. It's critical for those sharing prophecies to be connected properly within the Body of Christ and to be held accountable.

Once someone has established credibility and adheres to sound doctrine, we can measure what he prophesies against the Word of God. We can take note of the piece God is giving him and then listen to the different parts He's giving others in the Body. As we continue to search out the various pieces and put them together, what we see in part will start making sense in a greater context. The light will burst through the glass, and we can solve the enigma the Holy Spirit is highlighting to the entire Body of Christ!

QUESTIONS AND ANSWERS WITH RICK RENNER

In the program, Rick answered the following question from one of our viewers.

Q. Can a reprobate mind be reversed or is it permanent?

A. "My friends, a reprobate mind can be reversed. But what is a reprobate mind? The word 'reprobate' in Greek is the word *adokimos*, which describes a mind that is brilliantly fashioned by God but has been subjected to the bombardment of wrong images and information. All of that wrong information has twisted the mind, so it no longer thinks as God intended for it to think. It really thinks wrong but believes that it's right. That's why it's called 'reprobate.'

"Ephesians 4:22 says that we are to 'put off concerning the former conversation the old man, which is corrupt according to the deceitful lusts.' Then in verse 23, we are instructed to 'be renewed in the spirit of [our] mind.' If we will allow our mind to be bombarded by truth instead of wrong images and information, truth will reform our mind and renew it so we can begin to think in alignment with God's Word once again. It takes a strong decision to do this, but it means even a reprobate mind can be put back in shape."

STUDY QUESTIONS

Study to shew thyself approved unto God, a workman that needeth
not to be ashamed, rightly dividing the word of truth.
— 2 Timothy 2:15

1. First Corinthians 13:9 says, "For we know in part, and we prophesy in part." Prior to this lesson, have you ever thought about how prophecy comes in pieces here and there?

2. First Corinthians 13:12 says, "For we now see through a glass, darkly; but then face to face: now I know in part; but then shall I know even as also I am known." How did Rick's illustration of the Roman glass help you understand this verse better?

3. According to First Thessalonians 5:12, we are to know those who labor among us. How well do you know those who share prophecy on YouTube and social media? Do you know if they have a pastor, what their doctrine is, how they are connected to the Body of Christ, and if they are held accountable to others in the Church? If you don't know the answer to these questions, what should be your response to how you handle these prophecies?

PRACTICAL APPLICATION

But be ye doers of the word, and not hearers only,
deceiving your own selves.
—James 1:22

Learn to solve the prophetic puzzle in a biblical way.

1. What different prophecies have you heard that when brought together help paint a larger picture of the whole?

2. How are you esteeming others in the Body of Christ? Are you humble and cooperative, or do you pride yourself on knowing it all?

3. Have you ever caught yourself listening to an assortment of "prophecies" or "prophets" on YouTube? How are you using the Bible to discern what you are hearing?

Notes

CLAIM YOUR FREE RESOURCE!

As a way of introducing you further to the teaching ministry of Rick Renner, we would like to send you FREE of charge his teaching, "How To Receive a Miraculous Touch From God" on CD or as an MP3 download.

In His earthly ministry, Jesus commonly healed *all* who were sick of *all* their diseases. In this profound message, learn about the manifold dimensions of Christ's wisdom, goodness, power, and love toward all humanity who came to Him in faith with their needs.

☑ **YES, I want to receive Rick Renner's monthly teaching letter!**

Simply scan the QR code to claim this resource or go to: **renner.org/claim-your-free-offer**

Connect WITH US!

🏠 renner.org

f facebook.com/rickrenner • facebook.com/rennerdenise

▶ youtube.com/rennerministries • youtube.com/deniserenner

📷 instagram.com/rickrenner • instagram.com/rennerministries_
instagram.com/rennerdenise

www.ingramcontent.com/pod-product-compliance
Lightning Source LLC
Chambersburg PA
CBHW070757050426
42452CB00010B/1873